MW01130074

Sugar's Journey Home

Written by Stacy Snyder • Illustrated by Anne Johnson

Sugar's Journey Home. Ages 3-9.

For information please contact anne@wagdesign.be or stacysnyder@mac.com
First edition: USA 2022 ISBN: 978-0-9600041-2-6

This book is based on the true story
of two rescue animals who found each other
and became Best Friends.

Charger, the dog, had made it home after a long journey.
She had left Sugar behind with Sticker and Henry.

The Lady in the Red Hat was in her garden.
She was upset that Sugar and Charger were gone.
Her head was in her hands
and tears were running down her face.
She did not see Charger.

Suddenly,
she felt something on her cheek.

As she raised her head,
there was Charger,
licking away her tears.

The Lady in the Red Hat grabbed Charger and hugged her.

"Charger! Where have you been? I have been so worried about you. Where is Sugar?" she asked. Charger whined in distress.

"Okay, Charger, we will wait for her. I'm so happy you are home!"

Meanwhile, on the other side of the forest,
Sugar found her parents locked up in an old shed.
She paced anxiously—

—trying to decide when to set them free.

Sticker said, "Don't you think we should wait and ask the Moon and Sparkle when to go?"

Sugar impatiently replied,

"No, Sticker!
We need to leave NOW!"

8

"Sugar opened the door
to the shed with her nose.

Come on, Mom and Dad.
We need to leave."

9

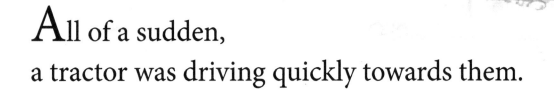

"They all headed out across a large, green, field.

All of a sudden,
a tractor was driving quickly towards them.

The tractor stopped in their path
and out stepped the Farmer.

Sugar was surprised!

Standing in front of her was the Farmer who made her haul firewood when her parents were taken away to perform.

2B-KIN

"AH, HA!" he said. "I remember you!
Now, I have three miniature horses
to haul my wood."

13

Sugar cried out to Henry the Hawk,
"Henry, please, help us!"

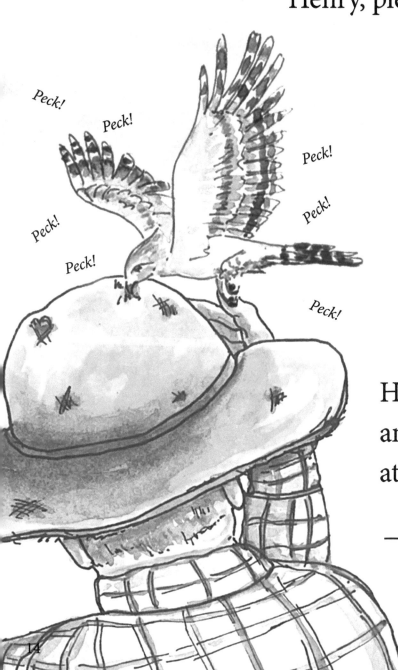

Peck!
Peck!
Peck!
Peck!
Peck!
Peck!
Peck!

Henry,
please help us!

Henry swooped down
and started pecking
at the Farmer's hat, —

— but the Farmer still
caught Sugar and her parents!

14

He tied them to his tractor and took them back to the shed.

Sugar hung her head.
She felt bad for not being patient.

"I am so sorry, Sticker!
We must wait for the Moon and Sparkle
to appear tonight and ask them what to do."

If only Sugar had listened!

"That night the Moon and Sparkle shone brightly down.
—They told Sugar and her parents not to frown.

Be patient, we will show you the way.
—You will all be home in one more day."

Sticker was hiding in the tall grass listening to the Moon and Sparkle.

The Moon said,
"Tonight you will see a ring around me,
which means there will be a light rain.

In the morning,
the sun will rise and welcome you with a beautiful rainbow.
Follow the rainbow to the giant tree,
and there you will find *your* 'pot of gold' ...HOME!"

19

That morning —

Sticker saw the beautiful rainbow appear
and knew it was time to move.

"Croo-aaaak!
It's time to move!"

21

Sticker found a tree stump
and launched himself into the air
to release the latch to the shed.

The door opened
and they began galloping
towards the colorful rainbow.

22

As Sugar and her parents were running away, they heard a loud rumble.

It was the Farmer.

—AGAIN!

Cranky the Crow, while quietly bathing,
heard Henry the Hawk cry out,

"Cranky, Please help us!"

Cranky flew away quickly

and moments later...

25

...He appeared with his crew of crows. They surrounded the Farmer and started pecking at the side of the tractor. There were crows everywhere!

The Farmer could not see where he was going—

— and drove straight into a ditch.

Sugar and her parents ran into the forest, following the rainbow.
They walked all day. Finally, just before nightfall,
they saw the magical tree in the distance.

Safely away from the Farmer, they could now rest.

That night when the Moon and Sparkle rose,
they all began to sing—

Thank you, thank you,
For all you do!

You freed us from
The Farmer too!"

The next morning was beautiful.

Birds were singing,

bees were buzzing,

and flowers were blooming.

Henry was flying ahead.

He could see the magical tree and just behind it–

–the house where the Lady in the Red Hat lived.

"We are almost there,"
chirped Henry.

33

As they rounded the tree, they saw the Lady in the Red Hat watering flowers with Charger. The Lady and Charger looked up—

—and they ran towards each other jumping, clapping, flapping and dancing with delight!

35

That evening,

— they looked up at the Moon and Sparkle—

— and said, "THANK YOU!"

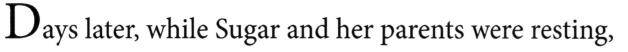

Days later, while Sugar and her parents were resting,

they heard someone driving down the gravel road.

Much to their surprise
they saw the Farmer.
They were afraid he had come
to take them back to his shed.

38

He got out of his tractor to talk to The Lady in The Red Hat,
who was not happy to see him.

39

After a long talk with The Farmer, the Lady told Sugar and her parents —

"The Farmer has something he wants to say."

The Farmer bowed his head and said,
"I'm sorry to have scared you. I want to be your friend
and treat you with kindness."

41

Relieved,

Sugar and her parents invited the Farmer

to stay the evening for a celebration with Sparkle and the Moon.

The new friends gathered that night around the fire

forming a circle of love while roasting marshmallows and telling stories.

They were so grateful to be together, forever, in their new home.

Life was REALLY good!

BEST FRIENDS!

LOVE!

FOREVER!

GOOD TIMES

FAMILY

MEMORIES

GOOD VIBES!

FRIENDSHIP

For Charger

Love, Charlie.

Now go back and see if you can spot any of these friendly little creatures.

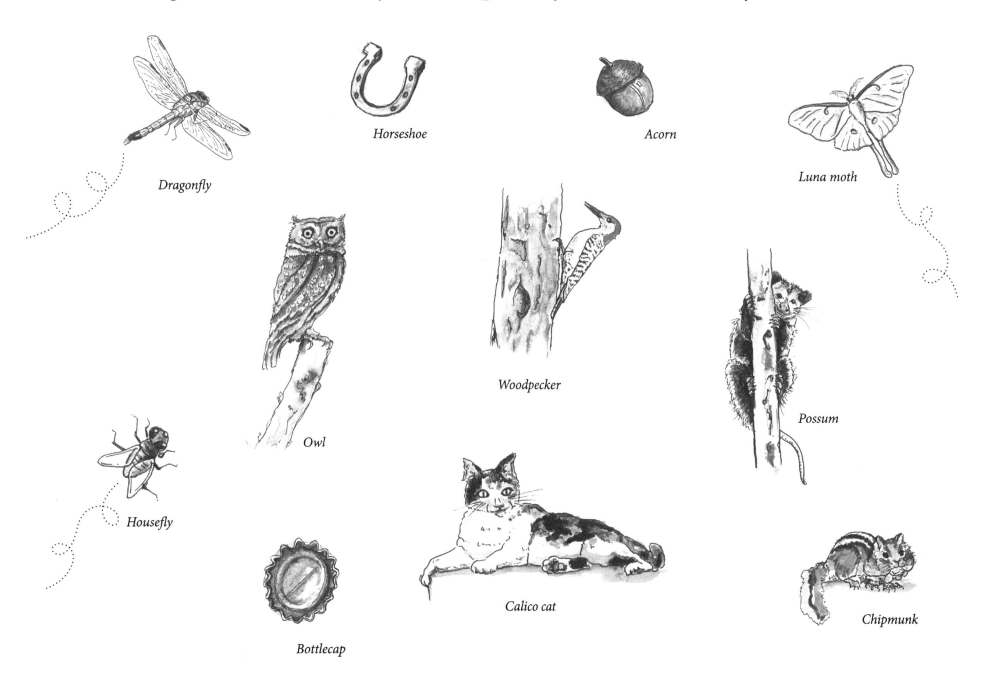

Dragonfly

Horseshoe

Acorn

Luna moth

Owl

Woodpecker

Possum

Housefly

Bottlecap

Calico cat

Chipmunk

STACY SNYDER is a graduate of the University of Arizona, with a degree in Special Education. She resides in San Diego California, with her loving husband John. She is the mother of two daughters, and the grandmother of four beautiful grandchildren. Her background in education and love for nature were the inspiration for this book. She was taken by the extraordinary relationship that developed between a rescued dog and a rescued miniature horse. Their unconditional love is a heart-warming example of kindness.

ANNE JOHNSON has held a career in painting, illustration and fine arts for over 30 years. She received a Bachelor of Arts degree from Roanoke College followed by a Master of Arts degree in Medical Illustration from the Medical College of Georgia, now Georgia Health Sciences University. She has an endless love for animals and nature and has been passionate about children's books since she was a young girl. After residing in Belgium for over 25 years she has recently returned to her hometown, Wayzata, Minnesota, and is the proud mother of three loving young adults, two dogs, a cat, and a horse. *Sugar's Journey Home* is her third book with Stacy Snyder.

SUGAR is a rescued buckskin miniature horse. She was in very poor shape when she was adopted. Scared and very skittish. With patience and spending lots of time with her, she has become a loving, contented horse with the help of her friend Charger. Age unknown.

CHARGER was adopted as a puppy, and had grown into a large, strong dog with a very happy disposition. Charger loved to go on walks with her best friend Sugar on a double leash. She also insisted on wearing sunglasses. Charger passed away peacefully in 2021 at the age of 12.

This sequel is dedicated to
the beautiful children, grand-children, cousins, nieces and nephews
that have all played an important part in its development.

Thanks to the loving support of this close-knit family
and the special bond between the author and the artist,
this book series is able to continue.

We would like to give special thanks to
the wonderful librarians of the Rancho Santa Fe Library
for their invaluable time, meticulous input and endless support.

CPSIA information can be obtained
at www.ICGtesting.com
Printed in the USA
BVHW090725221222
654780BV00001B/2